Needle Cra...

QUILTING

SEARCH PRESS
Tunbridge Wells

Introduction

Quilting is a very practical form of embroidery. It has been practised for generations. The original intention of sewing together two or three layers of material was to give warmth and protection. Soldiers wore quilted garments as a foil for arrows, and quilted jackets were worn beneath armour as a protection from the hard metal. Quilted petticoats and jackets were a great help in the days before central heating. A quilted bed-cover added warmth and richness to the furnishings of a four-poster bed. Many patchwork bed-covers were lined with an old blanket and quilted together, and the word 'quilt' came to mean a bed cover.

A modern sewing-machine makes quilting less time-consuming than in the past, though many people find the rhythm of sewing by hand very relaxing. If you have not done any quilting before, it is best to try out the technique with hand stitches.

Different types of quilting have acquired regional names (for example, English or Italian), but it is simpler to class them thus: *wadded quilting (English); corded quilting (Italian); shadow quilting; stuffed or trapunto quilting; flat quilting; padding.*

All forms of quilting are simple to work, but you get the best results from sewing with a good rhythm. This comes with practice so it is a good idea to work a small sample before you begin your first article. Tasks suitable for beginners are a baby's cot quilt, the front of a waistcoat and a shoulder bag (Although this booklet offers instructions on all methods of quilting no directions are given for making up items involving dressmaking and other techniques which are beyond its scope).

Natural materials are the easiest to work with, but with experience you will be able to quilt synthetics, leather and difficult fabrics such as velvet.

Quilted shapes used on a panel. The wadded quilting was worked by hand on a frame before being cut out; the edges were turned under, and applied to the panel by hand (*by Kit Pyman*).

Panel – 'Red Square'. The source of the design was photographs of buildings in Red Square in Moscow. Worked by hand in wadded quilting, using a frame, with added nets, lurex thread, and hand embroidery (*by Sheila Kinross*).

4

Wadded (English) Quilting

This is the most suitable quilting for a baby's cot quilt. It consists of a layer of wadding sandwiched between two layers of material and stitched together.

Fabrics

Choose a closely-woven material which is soft and pliable and gives a smooth finish. Pure silk, cotton poplin, fine linen, or fine wool all quilt well. Because the shadow cast by the depth of the quilting is a feature of this type of embroidery, pale colours are usually more effective. For a quilt or bag use a similar type of material for the top and underside, but for the front of a waistcoat you might use a thinner material underneath as this could form the lining. Choose a plain fabric or your design will be lost.

Printed fabrics are occasionally used. Here the stitchery follows the outline of the pattern, whereas commercially-quilted fabrics have a grille of straight machine stitch superimposed on the pattern. Further surface interest can be added with embroidery; for instance, French knots and eyelet holes, as in the fabric on the front cover.

Filling

Use a washable woollen or synthetic wadding, or an old blanket.

Design

Wadded quilting needs an all-over design so that the filling does not move around inside the two layers of material. Don't leave any large areas unquilted.

It would be dull to work a whole quilt in straight lines or diamonds, though it is a very efficient method of machine

quilting. Traditional quilting designs were simple shapes taken from articles found around the house and garden:
Feather straight or curled (*fig. 1*). *Fan* which could become a rose (*figs. 2 & 3*). *Spectacles* which become a chain for a border (*fig. 4*). *Wineglass* provides the basis for an all-over pattern to work as a background for the main design (*fig. 5*). Alternatively, a simple meander pattern can be very effective, as in the machine-quilted bag on page 30.

All-over patterns can be developed by using one or two simple templates (as above), starting at the centre and working out. The shapes can also be built up into squares or rectangles, or made into borders.

The charm of quilting derives from the play of light and shade on the 'puffed' areas which are light, and the flattened stitched areas which look darker. Keep this contrast in mind when planning a design.

Design sources

Paper cut-outs often suggest patterns for quilting. The design in *fig. 6* was based on a strip of paper folded in half with 'bites' cut out. The paper and the cut-out bits were then used as templates.

Photographs of microscope slides to be found as illustrations in many scientific books are another good source of patterns. The shapes in *fig. 7* were suggested by the cells of fossilized coral. To add interest, the centres of the cells could be worked as eyelet holes, and the little circles between the cells as French knots.

The trellis and flower pattern in *fig. 8* comes from a wallpaper pattern, simplified to these two shapes. A book of these wallpaper samples can be a useful inspiration.

Sculptures and bas-reliefs also translate well into quilting, as shown in the border on page 19.

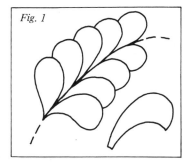

Fig. 1

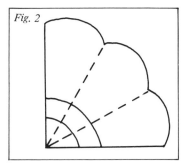

Fig. 2

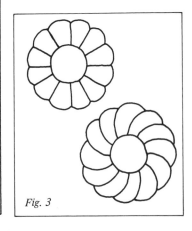

Fig. 3

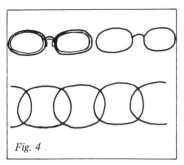

Fig. 4

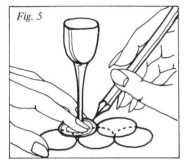

Fig. 5

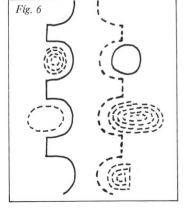

Fig. 6

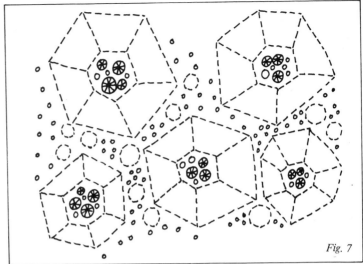

Fig. 7

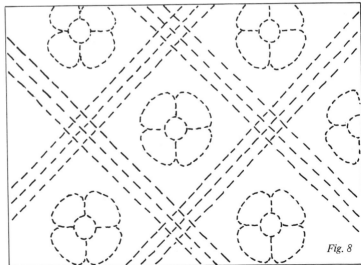

Fig. 8

7

Quilt. A project worked by a group, consisting of squares of wadded quilting with both hand and machine stitching and appliqué which were worked separately and then joined together. The design was inspired by the Cotswold countryside (*designed by Sue Rangeley, worked by members of the Embroiders' Guild, lent by Xonia Slade*).

Panel: 'painted rose'. The shape of a rose outlined in backstitch in wadded quilting, on a top fabric previously flooded with pink and green colouring (*by Barbara Anne Jones*).

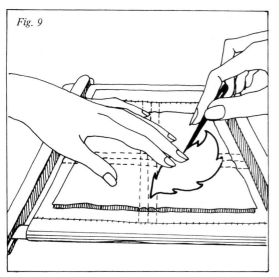

Fig. 9

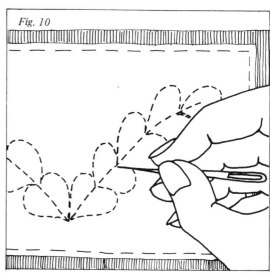

Fig. 10

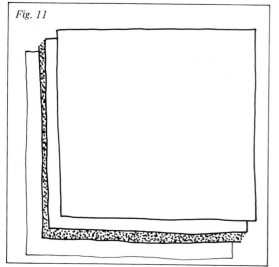

Fig. 11

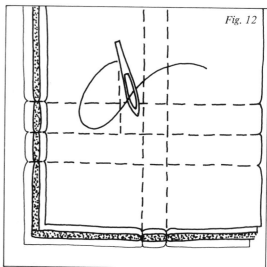

Fig. 12

Transferring designs

Begin by planning your design on a piece of paper. Iron the material now as you cannot do so when the quilting is finished. Then transfer the design to your top material, by templates or tacking.

Template method. Cut out templates for the main pattern shapes. Place these on the top material and mark round them either with tailor's chalk or, if you are using poplin or silk, with the point of a needle (*fig. 9*). If the needle point does not make an impression on the material you have chosen and you have to mark your design with tailor's chalk, you must tack over the chalk lines or you may find the design has rubbed off before you have finished working. All three layers should be prepared and tacked together before marking design on top fabric.

Always keep a copy of your design to refer to as you work.

Tacking method. This method may be used before the three layers have been tacked together. Draw the design on tracing paper. Place it on the right side of the material to be quilted. Tack along the line of the design with small running stitches, then tear away the tracing paper. If you draw the point of the needle along the line of the design, so that it slits the tracing paper, it will be easier to pull away the paper without disturbing the tacking stitches which form the design (*fig. 10*).

Preparations

Placing the three layers together (*fig. 11*). Place the underside material or lining on a flat surface. Spread the wadding on this, then the top material on the wadding.

Tacking or basting. Now tack all three layers of material together, starting from the centre and working outwards. Use a tacking thread which matches the material so that the tacked design still stands out (*fig. 12*). Put the needle in at the centre of the article and tack out to each side. Again start tacking from the centre and tack out to the top and bottom. Now tack about 1½" − 2" above the first line, then the same distance below until all three layers are firmly and evenly tacked together. You can tack small articles with rows of sloping stitches, but always start tacking from the middle (*fig. 13*). This preparation is very important, otherwise the layers will shift when you start to quilt and you will have creases where you don't want them. The top material can easily slide away from the wadding, particularly if you are using the machine. If the fabric is very delicate, use a fine needle (crewel 9/10 or a bead needle) for the tacking.

Threads

Use a matching coloured thread: cotton for cotton or linen, sewing silk on silk. A fine strong thread is best; it will sink into the folds of the material giving the soft padded effect which is the essence of quilting.

Matching coloured cotton thread is not always easy to find but a sewing silk works very well on cotton poplin, linen or fine wool as they are all natural fibres.

Framing work

Small articles to be hand-sewn need not be mounted in a frame. If a ring frame is used, keep the backing material taut, and let wadding and top material lie without tension. To frame up for hand quilting, sew the backing fabric only to the webbing at the top of the frame. Lay the wadding on top, then the top material with the design marked over the wadding. Now tack all three layers together as already explained. Tie a length of tape to the top left-hand corner of the frame and pin the tape to the material. Take the tape over the bar at the left-hand side of the frame and bring it back under the bar and pin again to the material. Continue to the bottom. Now pin the other side in the same way (*fig. 14*). It is best to use small safety pins for pinning.

Nest of boxes. Based on a patchwork template, padded, quilted, applied and embroidered. The design illustrates a perpetual calendar, each box representing two months of the year (*by Isobel Elliott*).

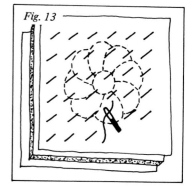

Fig. 13

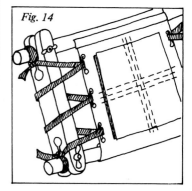

Fig. 14

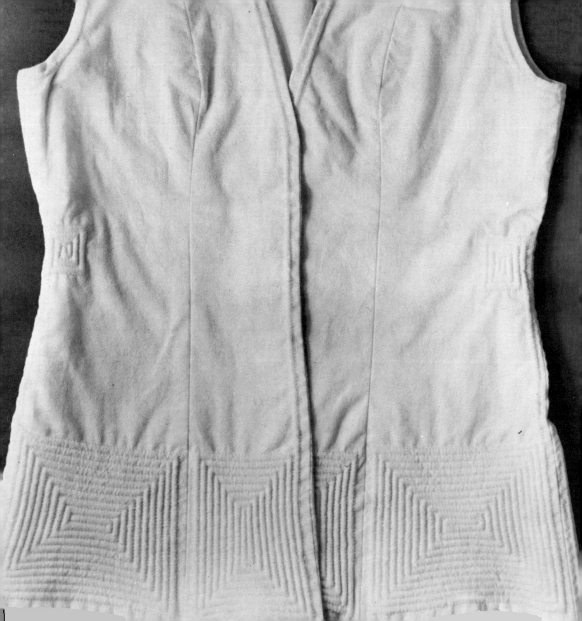

Jacket with corded quilting border.
The parallel lines were worked using the presser foot of the machine as a guide, stitching from the outside into the centre. The channels were filled with four strands of Aran knitting wool (*by Margaret Rivers*).

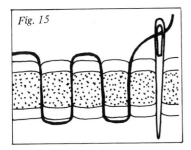

Fig. 15

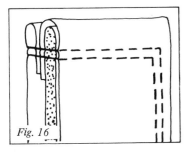

Fig. 16

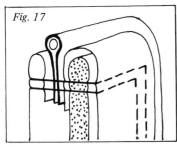

Fig. 17

Hand stitching

A running stitch is usual for wadded quilting. The stitches must be even but need not be very small; about 1/8" (3mm) is a good size. Make sure the needle goes right through the three layers. The stitches on the back should be the same size as those on the top. The stitch should be done in two movements: down through all three layers, pulled through, back up through all three layers (*fig. 15*). Start working from the centre.

Machine stitching

Small pieces can be worked in a ring frame. Larger pieces should be thoroughly tacked before sewing. Always start in the centre and work outwards. Use a straight stitch with length adjusted to the depth of fabric. Machine quilting is generally flatter than hand quilting. When machining lines over an area, such as the front of a jacket or a bag, stitch one half from top to bottom, and the other half from bottom to top. This evens out the 'pull' of the stitching.

Making garments

If you are quilting a garment or part of a garment don't cut out the pieces. Mark round the paper pattern pieces and cut out the garment when the quilting is finished. Remember the quilting will take up some material so allow an extra 1"−2" (25mm-50mm) when tacking round the dress pattern. When you have finished the quilting cut away the wadding from the seam allowance or you will have very bulky seams.

Finishing

To finish a wadded quilt turn in the edges and sew together with two rows of running stitches (*fig. 16*). If you prefer, finish with piping cord covered with a bias-cut strip of fabric inserted between the two layers of material (*fig. 17*).

CORDED (ITALIAN) QUILTING

Only two layers of fabric and no wadding are used in this type of quilting. It does not add warmth or bulk to garments, but is a useful way of stiffening areas of fabric, such as pockets and cuffs and the hems of skirts and curtains. It is often used with other forms of embroidery, and in the past was worked on fine linen to decorate bed linen, caps and petticoats.

Fabrics

Fine silks, satins, cottons and linen, soft leather, fine wool and synthetic suede are suitable fabrics. As in wadded quilting, choose a fabric with a smooth surface. The backing fabric is muslin, organdie, or sometimes fine cotton.

Design

The design is outlined in two parallel rows of stitching, usually about 5mm apart, forming a channel through which thick wool or string is threaded at the back, making the lines stand out in relief on the top fabric.

Designs should be kept simple and the curves smooth, as it is difficult to pad points and intricate curves. Long continuous channels make for easier threading.

Sources of ideas

Designs can be adapted from various sources. Wallpaper pattern books are a good source. Ideas for scrolling shapes can be adapted from patterns found in wrought iron gates, railings and fanlights — or books illustrating these. Geometric shapes can be worked out on graph paper; useful motifs could come from such sources as architectural illustrations.

Printed fabric bag. Wadded quilting lightly padded with terylene wadding. The lines of machine stitching augment the pattern of the fabric (*by Maureen Pallister*).

Transferring designs

These can either be tacked or chalked onto the top fabric, or traced onto the backing fabric.

Tacking method

In the same way as for wadded quilting, the design is drawn onto tissue paper or tracing paper and laid face upwards on the right side of the top fabric; the lines are stitched through tissue and fabric with a small running stitch. Then the paper is torn away. The lines can be worked over with a slightly heavier thread, or the tacking can be removed as the design is worked.

The design can be indicated with chalked lines, which are thick enough to be stitched at either side, forming a channel for the wool padding.

The design can be traced onto the fabric with a dressmaker's carbon, using the accompanying instructions (this is not always successful, as the marks do not rub out easily).

Tracing method

The design is transferred to the backing fabric, and the quilting is done from the back. Lay the piece of backing fabric over the design, and trace it off with a pencil. Lay the backing fabric on the top fabric and tack together, as for wadded quilting (remember that the design will be reversed by this method; that is, you will get a mirror image).

If worked from the back by machine, all the thread ends must be carefully pulled through to the back and finished off. If they are worked by hand, use running stitch, or chain stitch which will look like back stitch on the front (*fig. 18*).

Border in wadded quilting of three figures taken from a Pictish monument. Worked in backstitch by hand in a frame (*by Sheila Kinross*).

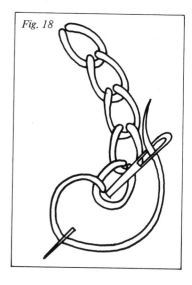

Fig. 18

Nautilus shell. Drawing of a shell which has been translated into two designs, one in wadded quilting and one in corded quilting with Trapunto quilting (*by Jane Clarke*).

19

Panel 'Rose'. Stuffed quilting techniques were used for this rose, worked on a dark green background in several ivory fabrics. The padding was terylene wadding; the petals were worked with straight machining, and embroidered with French knots, buttonhole bars and straight stitches (*by Jo Peterson*).

Free machining

It is possible to work rows of Italian quilting using the machine foot as a spacer. Start in the centre, having tacked the two fabrics together, and make a single line of straight stitch round a paper template. Use the width of the foot to work successive lines of straight stitches round this shape, forming the channels which are threaded with wool. Alternatively, blocks of lines can be worked in different directions. Remember to do the tacking beforehand in exactly vertical and horizontal lines. This will help to keep the stitching straight.

When machining a large area, work one half from top to bottom and the other half from bottom to top.

Method

Transfer the design to the fabric. Tack the top fabric to the backing fabric in the same way as for wadded quilting. When the design is worked, turn the quilting over to the back. Use a blunt needle and thick wool or string, and thread the padding through the stitched channels, pushing the needle through the muslin. Bring the needle out at intervals, and re-insert in the same hole, leaving a tiny loop (*fig. 19*). This will prevent the material from puckering and will work back into the rows of stitching. Never try to push the needle round a tight curve. Keep looking at the front of the work to see that the padding is even. If necessary, some channels may be threaded two or three times.

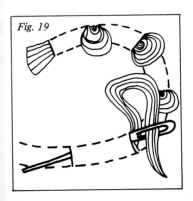

Fig. 19

21

TRAPUNTO OR STUFFED QUILTING

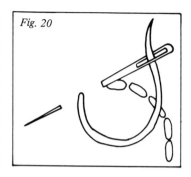

Fig. 20

This is another decorative form of quilting in which small areas are padded and stand out in relief. It combines very well with corded quilting, and is worked in the same way on two layers of fabric which are padded or stuffed after the design has been worked.

Fabrics

The top fabric should be smooth and soft. Make sure that the backing fabric is firm enough to allow the top one to plump up, otherwise the padded effect may appear underneath instead of on top.

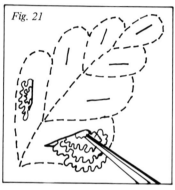

Fig. 21

Design

The designs for trapunto quilting can be bolder than those for corded quilting and are not kept to parallel lines. Trapunto is best worked on small areas, as large ones tend to look clumsy. The shapes should be kept simple as it is difficult to pad intricate shapes neatly.

Filling

You can use lambswool or synthetic wadding. The best filling for trapunto work is chiropody wool, available from chemists, which is springy enough to keep the shapes plumped out. Do not use cotton wool as it tends to become lumpy.

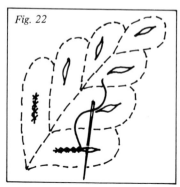

Fig. 22

Transferring designs

As there are only small areas, the template method is most often used if working from the right side of the work. Otherwise shapes can be traced on the backing material and machined from the back.

Method

Transfer the design either to the top fabric or the backing fabric. Tack the two fabrics together as described for wadded quilting. The design is worked in back stitch (*fig. 20*) or in straight stitch on the machine using a matching thread. Turn the work over and make a little slit in the backing material at the back of the area to be padded (*fig. 21*). Push in the filling with an orange stick or scissors point until the area is firmly stuffed. Sew up the slit (*fig. 22*).

Flowerhead. Shadow quilting with felt between organdie and backing (*by Valerie Harding*).

Lavender bags. Shadow quilting with felt between two layers of organdie (*by Kit Pyman*).

Evening bag. Corded quilting in heavy silk, machined in a contrasting thread from the back, following a pencilled design on the organdie backing. The cut-away shapes are backed with pieces of sheet sequin (*by Kit Pyman*).

CORDED SHADOW QUILTING

This is worked in exactly the same way as corded quilting, but the top and backing fabrics are transparent (for instance, organdie and chiffon), and the channels are threaded with brilliantly-coloured wools, silks or raffia.

SHADOW QUILTING

Areas as well as lines can be shadow quilted. Both top and backing fabrics are transparent, and shapes cut out from brilliantly-coloured non-fraying fabrics (felt, vilene, and so on) are sandwiched between the two layers and stitched closely round the outline, as on the two lavender bags on page 24 and the rose on page 23.

Evening skirt. A wadded quilting border worked on a wool skirt, heavily padded, with machine stitchery (*by Marjorie Barnard*).

PVC evening bag. An example of padding on a quickly-made design. The circles were marked round coins laid on the back of the pvc, which were laid over a pile of diminishing circles of felt and stitched down all round. The stitching is covered with lurex cord, couched down with invisible nylon thread, which is also used to sew on the beads (*by Kit Pyman*).

FLAT QUILTING

As the name suggests, there is no padding to give a raised effect with this type of quilting, but as two layers of material are sewn together, it can add warmth and substance to a garment, and weight the hem of a curtain. If a soft woollen material is used for the top fabric the stitching gives surface texture. Any of the fabrics recommended for other types of quilting is suitable for flat quilting, and with experience it can also be worked on synthetics, leather, real or simulated suede, velvet and so on.

Design

As the surface of the fabric is not rounded, the interest in flat quilting comes from the areas of plain fabric contrasted with the lines of stitchery, and the design should be planned with this balance in mind. A contrasting coloured thread could be used, or different thicknesses of thread. For instance, if using a cotton perle thread try using nos. 5, 8 and 12. The use of chain stitch would add weight to the important parts of the design.

Transferring designs

As with corded quilting, designs can be transferred onto the top fabric and worked from the front, or traced on to the backing fabric and worked from the back.

Method

Transfer the design, and tack the two fabrics together as has been described for corded quilting. Whether the work is to be machined or sewn by hand, it can be mounted in a ring frame. The most usual method of sewing the two fabrics together is by running stitch, back stitch (*fig. 20*), or chain stitch. Flat quilting is often combined with both corded and trapunto quilting.

Transfer-dyed cushion in wadded quilting. A pattern was splodged on to absorbent paper using transfer dyes. This was placed face down on the man-made fabric, and pressed with a hot iron. The design was then worked in wadded quilting (*by Margaret Hampson*).

Panel: 'Gryphon' in flat quilting in contrasting coloured threads (*by Nora Jones*).

29

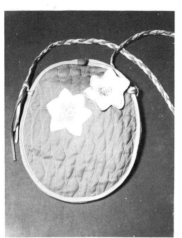

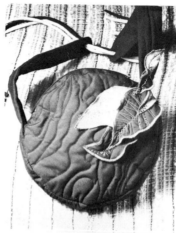

Silk evening bag with detached flower. Machine quilted with a double needle in contrasting threads. The flower is made separately, as described on page 31 (*by Sue Rangeley*).

Shoulder bag. Machine-stitched wadded quilting, with separately applied quilted flowers (*by Margaret Blow*).

Evening jacket. Machine quilted in Thai silk, padded with terylene wadding, backed with muslin, and lined with Jap silk. The centre shape was outlined in tacking and machined round with a straight stitch in a matching thread. The other lines are worked using the width of the machine foot, carefully starting each round from the tacked centre line at the top (*by Eileen Gregory*).

PADDING

This is not strictly quilting, but is sometimes used with or in addition to quilting. You can raise shapes by using layered felt. Cut the shape in the chosen material. Cut three or four pieces successively smaller in felt. Place the smallest piece on the centre of the shape; then the next pieces in size order; and then cover with top fabric and catch-stitch round.

QUILTED LEAVES AND FLOWERS

Lay the backing fabric on a smooth surface, cover with the wadding, then lay on the top fabric. Make a card template of the leaf or flower, lay it on the top fabric and chalk round. Pin the fabrics together and machine a line of straight stitch round the chalked line. Blow off the chalk. Make a zig-zag line round over the straight line. Cut out the shape. Zig-zag round the edge again (possibly in a different coloured thread) and the shape will curl and twist. Apply the quilted shape to the main piece of work with machine stitchery or hand embroidery.

ACKNOWLEDGMENTS

Edited by Kit Pyman
Text by Georgette Johnson, drawings by Richard Deacon
Photographs by Search Press Studios

Text, illustrations, arrangement and typography copyright © Search Press Limited 1978.

First published in Great Britain in 1978 by Search Press Limited, Wellwood, North Farm Road, Tunbridge Wells, Kent TN2 3DR

Reprinted 1982, 1984

All rights reserved. No model in this book may be reproduced for commercial purposes without the previous written permission of Search Press. No part of this book, text or illustration, may be reproduced or transmitted in any form or by any means by print, photoprint, microfilm, photocopier, or in any way, known or as yet unknown, or stored in a retrieval system, without written permission obtained beforehand from Search Press.

ISBN 0 85532 410 4

Made and printed by International Publishing Enterprises, S.r.l., Rome.

Front cover:
Printed fabric in which the pattern is outlined with running stitch in wadded quilting, with added knots and eyelets (*by Kit Pyman*).

Inside cover:
Waistcoat detail. Wadded quilting, worked on the machine, with an applied flower incorporated (*by Sue Rangeley*).

Back cover:
Panel: 'Wall with railings'. The corded quilting was worked first on the top fabric by machine. The backing, terylene wadding and top fabric were then framed up, and the wall worked by hand in backstitch and embroidery. Finally the flower eyelets were worked in the hand (*by Kit Pyman*).